Moment of Truth

by

Mounir R. Mkarzel

authorHOUSE®

AuthorHouse™
1663 Liberty Drive, Suite 200
Bloomington, IN 47403
www.authorhouse.com
Phone: 1-800-839-8640

First published by AuthorHouse 8/10/2007

ISBN: 978-1-4343-0826-9 (sc)

Library of Congress Control Number: 2007905326

Printed in the United States of America
Bloomington, Indiana

This book is printed on acid-free paper.

CONTENTS

INTRODUCTION

At a time when history has become what some politicians make out of it, or make believe it is.

At a time when people have to endure the conflict of politics with an open and an end projection politics aiming at confusing them with unfulfilled promises.

At a time when projected politics are conducted as if they were experimental politics.

At a time when experimental politics linger on, where is the truth?

It is pretentious to say we know it all. But it is equally pretentious to deny its existence.

Truth has its moment, and when it shows, it is self-evident. It goes from evidence to evidence.

It is a continuous procession of progress for the betterment of humans while experimental politics puts in doubt the evidence for what it is, and hence, the creation.

Throughout this book, I have tried to journey with people to the creator, the eminent truth of all.

The best believers of us are witnesses of the eminent truth.

I apologize in advance if I have offended any one, I did not mean to.

CHAPTER 1

The Benefit Of The Doubt

When an experimental policy is conducted and is not conclusive, the question that imposes itself is: "How much of the truth does it carry and what percentages of people are for it?

It is hard to figure out that it could carry more than 50%, otherwise it would knock on the door of democracy and trigger the self-evidence of the truth to come into play.

In order to fill in the gap to the 50% and become sustainable, it would need a substitute to democracy, and that is an authoritarian system of governing using the power to fill in the gap and repress people's discontent.

Such power has gone to seeking wars in order to make up the lack of majority rule. The difference between winning a battle and winning a war is not much contemplated by the dogs of wars, and the projected success of winning an ongoing battle blisters the pride of winning a war, otherwise "victory" would impose itself as a "truth", and "democracy follows." The more projected battles are conducted, the more blistering becomes a victory and thirsty and eager the dogs of wars.

From one battle to another battle, from one promise to another one, and the war expands and lingers on.

Never have the seekers of unlimited battles of war in order to promote their authority and fill in the gap to majority have ended by winning the majority of their people. So, they resent destiny and engage deeper in their experimental politics. It looks as if they were going through a malaise or absurdity that only their superiority syndrome could give relief to.

They establish themselves a breed above the rest. They become more equal than the equals and, hence, further themselves more from the truth.

The cults of their personality become their evidence of life, and since they can not offer the truth to people, they ask people to offer themselves to them, and endure the experiment they entered into.

The experimental politics become more penible until people would either vote against it or become vulnerable and doomed to a destiny of destruction to the extent that any revolution, as the last result, by the citizens becomes more weakened with the passing of time, and the country more vulnerable for lack of victory.

But until then, people are entertained to give that experiment another chance and in criminal legal words the benefit of the doubts before judgment already written and waiting to be declared.

The following becomes a declaration of defeat and remains that who would revolt against the defeat of the experiment and for the truth if people become doomed and fearful with one way out as defense mechanism, the benefit of the doubt?

A sovereign country has among other benefits the dignity and pride of its citizens. Its military protects and provides for the pride and dignity of a country and its citizens. Should a country loosen its grip to pride overseas with an increasing majority against the battles of war nationally, the question becomes how could the gap to majority be filled with the effectiveness of the use of power or force in decline?

When the ratio becomes two to one and the gap is still widening and people are doomed more and the more equals believe they are doomed less, the destruction of people and country becomes inevitable. History has proven that a substantial gap with no power success militarily to make up the difference is the bonkers of irreversible destruction.

Democracy is one moment of truth, it is the evidence of the power of people that no other experimental politics could substitute no matter what chances are given to the substitute or benefit of doubts is allocated.

CHAPTER 2

Democracy In The Making

In the beginnings of time, democracy did not exist, the use of force was the rule of the land, and this force could not be surpassed than by the force of miracles and hence, the birth of religions.

The first religion became the bastion of belief in one God, the Almighty.

The rule of law was necessary to implement the belief in God and the commandments were given.

And as well as miracles could not be the only way of life for humans, the rule of law would become the usual more acceptable way of life for humans.

The rule of law was given first in terms of commandments, from God to Moses, one-on-one.

Should the process of one-on-one be pursued in the making of the law, the deification of a human would dispirit and eclipse the human nature and seed its extermination.

The rule of law was brought to people who would gather and design or elect their representatives to enact into laws the various aspects of the commandments.

People became aware of God's justice and came to the belief that as it took the Almighty's intervention to set forth the basic principles of law, it would take his intervention to judge among people, and hence, people of God would apply justice. In another words, justice is given from God, through people who have bastioned the rule of law as their way of life.

Religion has expanded around the notion of justice.

Justice in turn has developed into every segment of population and path of life; the courts of law and the judicial system were upheld to the highest reach of democracy with the separation of powers.

What started to be people of God, in a sense of religious people, has expanded to become people of God, in a sense of common people, among them those who have taken law as their field of work to judge among people once designated by people.

This transitional phase marks the social pact among people and the integration of religious start into social end.

And justice is for all, regardless of religious differences.

Does it mean that God's hand, which took a human hand to write down the basic rule of law, has finished its work?

Certainly it has not. It means that the laws have developed with the progress to an extent that specialization is needed to reflect the divine purpose in every field of life. The judiciary is more and more populated by its own specialized people prepared to render decisions in the courts of law.

The development of democracy centers on the separation of powers, with each and every power becoming more and more equipped and accessible to handle its requirements according to the speed of the progress it acquiesces and promotes.

The obvious question that imposes itself is how much has each branch of government been populated and teamed with the progress in comparison with other branches of government?

If there is a disparity, for example, between the legislative and the executive, as to the number of human resources affected to their needed task, then one would have an edge on the other one, for it has more preparedness and readiness, it is more equipped.

In a presidential election year, wherein one issue galvanizes the electorate, if the executive branch is more or better equipped with more power than the legislative which represents the majority opposing the executive branch policy, both would most likely stalemate because they edge on each other, in a struggle between votes and power.

In this context, nor could the executive branch fill in the gap of popularity with the successes of battles, neither could the legislative power engage taken advantage of a majority it shares. Democracy seems to be in recess.

And the majority needs more majorities and the power for war needs more powers and the disengagement goes on.

And what was the war for a country becomes a regional one, and from regional to the world, where the hope for success could be more debatable, only to find out that democracy in recess does not win wars, or reaches successes on any scale.

CHAPTER 3

The Give And Take

A stalemate in a democracy is not permissible nor is it affordable. Democracy is a big receptacle of opinions, issues and attitudes that are streamlined in a reflective evidence of the truth and life among people.

Democracy is a challenge for betterment centered on a pledge for country and God.

The Founders understood this intimate relation between God and country, they used the word "perfect" to emphasize this relation, in the more perfect union, added to it "under God." They developed a theme of perfection that could eventually lead to a junction through an aspiration to the Almighty.

An Almighty, with the force of miracles, helps win over the force of destructions and hence helps democracy.

So one can't go against democracy without going against God, and can't go against God without going against democracy. The bond has been established. And it is clearly mentioned in the oath of office of the president: "So help me God."

Some scholastics would want to see a competition going between the allegiance to the country and the appurtenance to a religion on the grounds that God manifests himself through religion.

Those scholastics could not understand, and if they do, could not admit that the Constitution is not competing with the Bible or Koran or others, and the American people are believers in God, and the United States is the superpower of the world not despite God's help but because and with God's help.

Some scholastics take that competition as a positive one, others as a negative one to the extent that one can't live with the other.

And the real difference between denominations becomes mainly the difference between and among appurtenances on one hand and an allegiance on the other.

The appeal of God to people is for them to take that journey alive to him, becoming thus for a more perfect union starting with the humans who are called upon to God since their childhood. "Let them come to me," said Jesus, and adulthood is in no lesser of an appeal. We believe that God wants people alive and not dead, wants them determined and committed to go to him and not short of any other alternative in an assumption of death, a moment of truth opened to speculation, he wants them vibrant with moving life to his call, the everlasting truth, the undeniable pursuit, the journey to eternity.

We believe that God wants people to take that walk to him alive together and not dead against each other. That journey starts with birth, only an infant cannot walk, he has to be trained to the walk to eternity and be born again if he missed the first training until he can definitely do it on his own, becoming self-responsible. It is the gathering of the self-responsible in the belief in God that signals the beginning of the journey to the creator from this Earth. It is, indeed, that collective movement that makes God to be the third to every two gathered in his name.

There is no collective death movement, and there is no chariot to be carried, there is everyone for himself and God for all because the joy to meet him at a closer distance every day overcomes every other joy. That journey is not a ride in the reef, and forced death does not cut that distance. It is an earned journey for the deserving and determined people who have learned how to sweat to earn their living and cross that distance known only by him.

The collective movement of people in the long walk to their creator makes them win over the endurances of the walks of life, they embrace their pursuit, the one of the real believer with patience, and never give up on that ultimate opportunity since they have never missed on any other opportunity, in particular their land of opportunity, one settlement of believers before the everlasting one.

Helping them in their pursuit is the witness of people movement, a bystander, as have been every God's helper of people to witness people's march to God. The helpers are witnesses of the truth.

The helper is no maker.

The helper is no provider.

The helper is no heaven gate opener.

The helper is no taxicab carrier.

The helper is a witness of the truth; the life of people engaged in their pursuit to their creator, and also a witness of death of one or another individual whose life has tired him of being booked out of the mass and wanted people to carry him for he thinks he has the secret word to heaven. Each and every person is walking himself, and they are walking together, shoulder to shoulder, and no place for exception.

All people are created equal, and there is no place for the more or less equal in heaven.

And so, those who believe they could be more equal become the disabled of the faith. They need a ride, except that there is no motorized faith in the people's march to their creator.

There are miracles of the faith to lead to the observance of the law and not the destruction of it, with the use of force to offset the rule of democracy.

There is the rule of law as God has laid down, and we are all under, no one is above, and we are in it together, and togetherness implies a nation and hence an allegiance to the nation and not an appurtenance to a fragment and the fragmentation of the nation. The spirit of a country is adamant to fragmentation for the country is one, indivisible.

Should the force of miracles and belief leading to democracy be overplayed by other forces, then we have to ask for more miracles and more belief to sustain the miracles, otherwise we are stuck to accept a doomed destiny for doomed people moved by doomed destruction in order for the non-democratic forces to score and stay above people.

Doom and destruction, and vice versa, are in a cause-and-effect relation, and they serve the purpose of the wheeler-dealers of people; this is what the merchants of people believe in.

Would the wheeler-dealers compromise?

They give the impression of doing it, and here branches their sheer hypocrisy.

Wheeler-dealers of people know that people will not compromise on their destruction percentage-based politics. People are against their destruction whatever percentage there is.

So, there is no give and take compromise on the part of the people, but remains the remnant special interest group, a bizarre group of people tempted to do it again. And the politics of triggering and camouflage follow up.

In a democracy, people reach for their more perfect union, it is a steady drive, everyone brings in his share and accepts the other, and together they build a better future.

In getting better, people have every reason to agree together, but in getting worse, people have every reason to disagree among themselves, and it is the one that destroys more that gets an edge in a destruction derby race. When people become doomed to their destruction, the ones that know how to destroy them worse believe they would win the race. But they will not, God is not helpless, is not hopeless. He is the help and the hope against destruction at any grade, level, or rate.

CHAPTER 4

The Special Group Of Interest

It is obvious to say that the special group of interest does not revere the Constitution and what it stands for. It is always looking for a subterfuge, only the subterfuges melt down in the big receptacle of people after having inflicted some harm and damages to people.

The reasons of the meltdown are many; among them are the tenacity, patience, determination, and endurance of people to face their responsibilities because they believe in God and country. The other reasons of equal importance are the different groups among the people that do not want the one special group of interest to prevail. These different groups have the leverage of people gathering not to engage in the schemes of differences of race and denominations among themselves.

And here looms the real danger of the special interest group that wants to split between the people and with the country in order to engage them separately after reaching for the power to make up the difference between their minority and the majority of people.

This danger would ineluctably culminate in a threat to the nation should the special interest group become a clear-cut religious denomination with a clear-cut hold on power.

Nothing is wrong with one denomination or another, what is wrong is a religiously oriented denominational interest group with their denominationally oriented politicians. At that time, nor would that special interest group accept to melt in the receptacle of democracy, although it knows it has to, neither would the other groups accept that the one special interest group would be the only group.

A negative confrontation would be waiting to challenge democracy directly. A democracy that has been held with the help of God, such a precious help that the forces of power abuse and special interest group and other groups never ended challenging its miracles, one way or the other. It is when they challenge themselves and need more miracles for democracy to win, that they will find out that democracy does not survive by the forces of miracles only, but also by the rule of law, and the supreme law of the land is the Constitution.

Then they will know the losses that they inflicted on people and country. Unfortunately, some are already trying to discount it, cashing in on it.

A country born less than 250 years ago became the superpower of the world, for it was designed to become so by its Founders that wrote its Constitution that substantiate in a small document in content but one of the greatest in reaches, meanings, and values, the connection between God, people, and country.

It proclaimed a divine purpose by responding to the appeal of divinity to have people come to it from all over the world; people in need will find comfort; people who hunger and thirst will find food and water; people who are oppressed, neglected, and rejected will find refuge, justice, freedom, and liberty. Blessed are those people for the kingdom of the United States is theirs.

A country next to God, lover of God, and love of God, not even the space of an arc has the Constitution afforded between God and country, from one leg to the other. The connection was made, stamped, and sealed. God bless America and help America.

The nation was conceived and the delivery was in its more perfect union.

The special group of interest disrupts the normal evolvement trend to a safe reach. It is not in tune with the pulse of the nation, it has no place in the nation. It could not be but imported, and therefore, it is not legitimate.

Such imported illegitimacy is coveted with the local and personal politics, the politics of the wheeling-dealings, and what is illegitimate for the country becomes legitimate for some politicians who are eager to win elections, bouncing forward and backward, stretching themselves to a dual confrontation between allegiance and appurtenance, enticed by extremism appurtenance as the dominant politics and as if people's votes are for sale, and worse than that a sale for an illegitimate cause under a brand of religion hospices.

Short of finding its legitimacy in the allegiance for the country, the special interest group resorts to an appurtenance to connect to a portion of the people as plea bargain and so does in turn that appurtenance to the special interest group.

Who is guiltier, the special interest group or the appurtenance-based politics, becomes the benchmark of politics. In the meantime, and until people impose themselves, the allegiance has to endure destruction and people have to accept their doomed situation.

What is illegitimate in its importation could not become legitimate by its consumption. The separation of church and state is proclaimed by the people except that there are extremists that in order to secure their highest apparatus in country and religion would try to transition from religion to country and vice versa, giving the non separation between state and church one try of success after another at the expenses of the nation..

The clash between extremists themselves would become inevitable. It is the clash among the apparatus highs. And in order to secure an upper hand, the extremists compete for the political power and the wheeling-dealing on the expense of the country gets more under way.

Religious extremists have made out of their respective religions a political and economical power play in order to make up for the lack of social mission they encountered, diverting thus for furthermore from the social mission religions are for.

The lack of a social mission is due in part to a global social life that has developed at a path and speed that made it increasingly harder for religions to communicate among each other in a mood of political rivalry. The catch to sustained rivalry to dominate the socio-political arena has moved the strain of endurance into a complex mix of politicians, laypeople, and clerics steered by vanities of extremism in some denominations.

In that mix, it is obvious that the Caesars of politics cannot win over the faithful in God, and it is equally true that the Pharisees of religions cannot win over the observers of separation of church and state. And what is applicable to church is applicable to temple, mosque, and synagogue and other sacred places of worship of God.

So who is the winner?

Time has never stopped proving that the winner over destruction is God.

Jesus wanted people to follow him as winners over death, and start their journey to the Almighty, his father, alive from this earth as he did.

Who would people choose?

Would they choose the Caesars, the Pharisees, or Jesus?

It is obvious that people have over the years chosen Jesus. People know how to pick a winner when they see a winner. The Caesars and Pharisees are things of the past, no matter how they gather in a special interest group. People of the United States have made up their mind perfectly clear, declaring that we the people … want a more perfect union under God. Also people of the world have found in Jesus a refuge and a lightning road to the truth.

The wheeler-dealers of politics, in order to make believe that they are not losers, disrupt the lightning and the refuge to Jesus so they try to reverse the truth, imploring religion extremists to sustain the death and killing of people.

And the more death of people is implored, the more people become doomed as if this is their infallible destiny.

People that have treasured the self-evidence of the truth have cherished their treasure so much so that no one can take it away from them because they want to be winners, the win of the king of peace, and the journey to the creator is revealed to rise over and again.

CHAPTER 5

The School Of Politics

The interest special group politics together with a religious appurtenance-based politics have been a lucrative association, or so it promises, and, therefore, has had a ripple effect among some politicians that had to compete to win the prize. Such competition has indulged the country in an era of silent movement of disturbances to the Constitution and what it stands for, one nation under God.

The honeymoon between the special interest group and the denominational appurtenance politics disturbed not only the politics but also the social and economical life of the country to the extent that the prize of winning the special interest group reward became conditioned on the more spread of the various disturbances in different fields of life.

This process of disturbances has been encouraged so much so that the more disturbances there are, the better are the rewards. It has been a long process until the culmination from disturbances to destructions and all the way to renewed wars to the extent of which that should a divorce happen between the special interest group and the denominational brand of appurtenance politics, the ripple effect that their congenial life was felt on the new generation would be felt for a long time, and would grow, if not addressed properly, to become a life crisis.

This school of politics had swirled from the Constitution; its merits and values, spirit and pulse. It has brought to people a relic of deviation from the right track and an absurd unknown future opposing the customary way of life, the social bond and fiber, family and institutions.

Our young generation is now faced with an uncertainty of success in life that is widening as much as the gap between old and young generation is widening, the connection is loose, and the blame is strong, each generation blaming the other one for the lack of togetherness and the denial of each other.

Where is the truth that gathers people around it?

The truth is God.

Everything comes and goes. He does not. He is always there, has always been, will always be from generation to generation. He is the eternal being on Earth and in the infinite.

The problem of the generation gap centers on the being. One sees it real and true in God, the giver of life, from one generation to the other one, and one is looking for it in a godless world, an unknown world at best.

And the question becomes the following:

If God does not fill in the gap, who does it?

It is obvious to say that the presence of God is felt and the number of people admitting him is growing constantly, embracing almost the whole planet Earth.

This admission has been in a continuous motion spreading knowledge of God.

Among the beholders of God's love are Moses, who carried the Ten Commandments to humans; Jesus, who made the flow of love and peace the milestone of the belief in God; and Mohammad, who understood the real life of Jesus, an eternal love of the Father God until a sad crucifixion by the humans, no matter what happened later, it did not come from humans. There is Jesus, an example to enlighten people if all of them could be enlightened, but not all of them could. And so the sword was used against the unenlightened who have abused the love of God either by negating him or making believe that the love of Jesus and his sacrifice and pardon would carry everyone and all to heaven regardless of their reluctance to go to God during their lifetime.

We believe that there is no faith by proxy as there is no motorized faith. We earn heaven; we do not take it for granted under any circumstances.

And those who do not need force to believe in God and are in peace with him, could they limit their faith into fighting others for the belief in God as if it is a dogfight over the same catch or should they in turn become a living example of an aspiration to meet the promoters of faith, God beloved ultimate responders to the Almighty call?

Brothers in faith should not fight each other, the better of them are the ones that knew how to aspire to providers of faith of the other ones without confusing between providers.

The aspiration to providers of faith is a key move to peace. Moses has laid down the rules of aspiration by transmitting the Ten Commandments. This is the peacemaker approach and needs not the rigid religious breakthrough from the lack of aspiration to prove one's faith in God and peace.

The schools of politics that want to replace Moses by extremist Judaic politics, and Mohammad by extremist Islamic politics, and Jesus by extremist Christian politics are missing the aspiration necessary to make peace, and resorting thus for to the lack of it to erect religion and faith on cataclysm politics and the like, as if Moses, Jesus, Mohammad and others are fighting in heaven and with no mercy. They are not.

CHAPTER 6

The Kidnapping Of The Truth

The Christian politics had recently positioned itself as the American politics despite the fact that the Constitution has opposed the meltdown of state and church, and what was the Christian politics is becoming more the American politics projected to engage within its ranks and with other denominations not on a better and more perfect nation under God, but on arm-to-arm basis, diluting thus for any merit to the aspiration of perfection, encouraged to do so by the enigmatic of dilution, the merchants of politics who find themselves blaming each other and the country for what they infused people with to let them do in error.

The error itself is against the truth, and correcting the error is tantamount to the truth. The error, if excused but not corrected, generates more errors. Everybody knows for sure that a religious denominational fight is an error. The war, for whatever excuse it invokes, if it does not correct the error, the excuses persist and so does the error, and in order for more errors to persist, the excuses have to persist and more of them. So the excuses become an inducement into more errors and the masters of inducements are no believers.

And from one inducement to another, the belief in God is attacked because of the differences among denominations believing in him. Such differences are exacerbated by the ongoing war.

The one among other differences is between the extremist Christian politics and the extremist Islamic politics. It has bewildered the minds since the American politics and the Christian politics have been described as if they were marching together, while the differences exist among the Christian denominations as well as the Moslem denominations leading the reasons for war.

Should the American politics be continuously projected, viewed, considered and consumed as if it were and will be the Christian politics, it simply would have to give up on its borders and its land to become global. It will become a dogma politics, leading to the negation of itself in the pursuit of a borderless entity and identity since it could not replace or act as if it were Jesus, the disciples, and ultimately God's justice hand in the promotion of justice in the globe, a prerequisite condition for peace, freedom, liberty, and equality among people.

It is equally true that the unpractical metamorphosis of Islam into any Moslem country and Judaism into Israel makes that country or the other lose its grip on its borders and become open to an abstract of ideologies and borderless conceptions of social politics.

The question becomes: Who among those dogmatists of a kind will pay most the price of losing its borders' grip?

It is obvious that the more extremist a country becomes, knocking on God's door, the more vulnerable it becomes, especially if it has merchants of people, since what is at stake is the dooming of people and the rising of the few extremists on the ruins of destruction. And the more destruction thereof, the more doomed people are. And this phenomenon is due to become contagious.

The Constitution of the United States has secured the country from indulging into the one-sided dogma politics, raising above the differences of appurtenances, and among them the extremism appurtenance on extremism-based politicians. The wisdom of its Founders should not be overshadowed by the outburst of destruction to serve sectarianism's end. It is against the sanity of the people that have been raised to savor the wisdom of their Founders and not to drill the sweet anger of imported sectarianism that the wheeler-dealers are vehemently laboring to set basis now and more of it in the future, seizing the special interest group power-play politics to offset their popularity contest failure.

And when in the course of perturbing the socio-political order, they stumble on the barriers set forth by the Constitution, one nation under God; they either pick the nation or God to side with, but never both.

The merchants of politics, in order to secure the doomed status of people so they could use them as commodities, never have gone for God, people, and country; on the contrary, they have sunk themselves into being the divider between God, people, and country. And their power play makes them get away the next day with their disturbances of the public interest and order, as if nothing happened the day before, encouraged to do so again and again in a repeat performance of another kind, but always trying to make believe into the other way around.

Never have the merchants of politics lost sight of the immense progress and accomplishments this country has made with God's help, contemplating every opportunity they could grasp to reverse the progress. These grasped opportunities never fully presented themselves until the resurgence of the war in succession of the peace-making politics, as if the reason for war is peace and as if peace has one primary role and that is to promote war, the extended arm's-length philosophy of terrorism. So the maneuverings for war era were begun after the world had enjoyed peace for many years. These maneuverings came on in such a precipitous and contiguous way that it is shaping now as if it is an uncontrollable destiny, or so the merchants of politics want it to be.

It is that precipitous mode taking people by the surprise of tomorrow's wars against the serenity of yesterday's peace; war that has been set as a trend of the future, taking into account the power play of politics as if it is the chance of a lifetime, to the extent of which that the voice of the people is not heard any more and the party that was empowered for war is not posed for its political survival and no matter if it were ... as if the inducements into errors might have their day in politics kidnapping the truth and the belief in one God for all the people.

CHAPTER 7

The Wheeling-dealing Politics

The merchants of local politics need the wheeling-dealing with a broader, organized, and global power group, powerful enough to engage with them for their personal special interest.

This broad global group of influence has to be, in turn, motivated enough to draw down the public interest in favor of the special interest using those merchants of politics for a profit to be advanced and shared on the expenses of the common people.

Is that broad group of influence an organization or a country?

It is an organization as far as that organization could not be located and effectively targeted, and it is a country as far as that country could work in the dark and not be caught red-handed. So it is a mixture to start with.

Then it becomes more sophisticated with the passage of time when the local merchants of politics would have found themselves well versed into the wheeling-dealing politics disguised under the camouflage accession to fame, prestige and power grip.

With that accession, the organization's role starts to fade away in some given circumstances while the country's role replaces it, and vice versa, and the story goes on until proof of the contrary.

The trend in both organization and country against the superpower is the same in that it is one of accrued damages when the local wheeler-dealers in the superpower are still going on and audaciously going through with the next day as if nothing went wrong the day before.

It is a shame that entering the twenty-first century, it is still true what George Washington had rightfully said, that people have to endure some of their politicians. It is more so when that endurance becomes hopeless and helpless with the help and the hope of the wheeler-dealers, the merchants of politics with people as disposable commodities.

The spirit of the United States is unique in that it has provided the people with a unique commander in chief, George Washington, and a unique set of Founders who came up with a Constitution for politicians to follow on condition of always attaining for a more perfect union under God, like an eagle roaming the sky with a majestic pride and dignity going higher and higher every round, the sky the limit.

George Washington became president doing politics as a unique and proven successful commander in chief who had conquered the politics of endurance cautioning against it.

The other Founders have manifested their determination to engage in the making of the union on a collegial basis under the roof of a congress not conquered by the politics of endurance since it was designed by George Washington to attain for a more perfect union under God.

It is that collegiality that has read the future of the country by writing it down in a document called the Constitution.

A document never intended to be a sacrosanct book, although it is so close to it.

A document by the name of the Constitution is opened to the readers and closed to the writers unless they confirm its letter and spirit in the making of the more perfect union and unless the balance of power between the branches of government is disturbed for such a perfectionism goal set by the Founders needs such a successful commander in chief set by George Washington.

And then what if a George Washington or a good president and commander in chief is not around, should that more perfect nation goal under God and what pertains to it in the Constitution be altered or should the power given to one man be amended?

It is obvious that the choice should not exist since the head of the executive is bound to reach for the more perfect union, with God help, to bring the other branches of government to follow course, otherwise he is in default and his powers should be altered in order not to touch the goals of the more perfect nation under God set by the Constitution, for no man should be given so much power at the risk of subduing the country to his unpopular performances opening the way for the wheeler-dealers to trade against people and country on the assumption of who needs people and country since they got the president.

And before we know it, the gap between the president and people widens, people are asking for a better, more perfect union under God and a commander in chief that can't deliver, among other things, victories if he is for and became faced with a war. And then the profit takers will indulge the president himself to impose him as political commodity on a pay as you show basis, no one is spared.

CHAPTER 8

With God's help

Amidst that growing divergence resulting from unfulfilled promises of victories teetering on the edge of defeat, the Constitution steps in to trigger the safety valve it has provided people with. It is the pledge made to God and country that comes to the rescue, the pledge of believers in God asking him to deliver them from defeat and their country from destruction.

And God will not turn his back on his believers and will not let their country down for in God they trust. At the time God's help is needed and given, the truth got its moment no matter how the nonbelievers would look at it, as if it is an act of belligerence against a commander unfulfilled promise of victories. God's help, among other things, will help correct the course of failures before they stack up and consume the country, even if it takes a change in the commander's preferences one way or the other.

Most of the people in the country are saying it is wrong to stay in Iraq. Their decision binds their politicians. It is not a solicitation that the people are making to a commander in chief in order for him to decide on the merit of the people's case.

In a trend of an Iraqi war that has taken a bad turn to the worst, every day counts and this war should not be construed as if it is a United State local fight between the hawks of war and the doves of peace with no stoppage in sight, and with billions spent and others changing hands in a wild market of green and blood where the realities are stolen and converted into fictions as if we had seen nothing yet but the tip of the iceberg and the worst is to come no matter what people want.

It is in that bondage of God and country that people feel their defense, for the Almighty is not helpless and hopeless nor should be the people that believe in him, otherwise the belief becomes self-defeating.

No one knows this self-evident truth more than the merchants of politics, but because they are merchants they politicize everything in order to wheel and deal about everything and hence they have a hard time admitting this self-evident truth as if the more they bargain with the evidence, the more politicized it becomes and the less self it will be.

God's love and help is no bargaining chip in order that the lesser its price is on the market, the more vulnerable it becomes to a takeover, trying to deprive people thus from the real love, help, hope, and trust and leave them unattended to a takeover by the so-called pretenders.

God forbid we turn away from him.

God forbid we do not rejuvenate and perpetuate our trust in him.

God forbid we turn our back on our moral values and Constitution.

The Almighty is all love but beware who, under the cover of embracing him, want to steal his love and sell it to people to make a profit out of it.

And since God's love is no bargaining chip that the merchants of politics can deliver to people, they resort to a stand-in position between God and people, taking away the people's chance to their direct journey alive to God.

And since to keep using people as if they were commodities of last resort, they develop an accrued interest in dooming them without real help or so they hope.

And since to keep people doomed, destruction is the recipe.

And since the more they destroy, the more doomed people become.

And since their ideals of politics have become doom and destruction, no wonder why things go from bad to worst.

Those who have seen themselves a breed apart above the people seem to have made up their mind to conquer divinity and humanity, fighting them both, relying on Lucifer, imploring him to let them win once so that they will control the universe. But the direct bond between people and their creator has been established by the Constitution, among other sacred books delivering them from harm.

Is the United States' Constitution a sacred document?

The Constitution is sacred for in God it trusts, and also is untouchable by the perpetrators of public disturbances and harm. And as much as that trust is fortified, it will remain the sacred document of the land. Having said that, what if this well-established trust is somehow shaken with the merchants of politics trying to politicize the help of God and challenge people's rights to God and country from their grasp of power triggering?

The Constitutionalists would advocate the possibility of amending such power that challenges the will of people, and the merchants of politics will then stop triggering and courting such power.

Such an amendment would have been welcome at the time the Founders were alive except that the presence of George Washington among them made it inappropriate and unnecessary because his devotion to his country was unequivocal, let alone the fact that he was and stayed the victorious commander in chief.

With today's filibusters being around, requirements and the compromise, the prerequisite of an amendment, becomes lost, and such an amendment would stay wishful thinking.

Does this country need, today, another George Washington that could order the wind and conquer the White House?

Or does this country need another set of Founders?

The latter is not contemplated.

Could this country turn to God's help, the safety valve of the Constitution?

This is quite affordable and knowledgeable by the people but not easily admitted by the merchants of politics and their connectivities.

Then what can this country do?

Should its president be more triggered by the special interest group of wheeler-dealers, the merchants of politics, then the country's militants in Congress and the goodwill people, together with God's help, have to stand together against dragging down this country.

CHAPTER 9

The Rescue Operation

When this country is put in the middle of a battlefield where the belligerents fighting each other have to fight this country stuck in the middle and its special group of interest not willing to pull out from this strategic error.

And when this middle position in between squeezes the country and shrinks its virtual and potential power,

And when its people are tucked in a position they do not like nor have they approved it as if raped by contumacy,

The country weakens itself and defeats its purpose of freedom of choice and become vulnerable to the contenders and competitors to its power, and the call is thrown in the political wilderness of an incoming prey.

When the pride and dignity of the people who have exemplified these standards of life is blemished,

And when its men and women in uniform lack adequate respect and dignity and proper treatment,

Then the call for a rescue reaches the skies and beyond, and the people who have calculated in their Constitution for the search of the Almighty, would not be alone for God's help is there for them, and they are good in calculus the goodness of believers trusting him with all their assets that the merchants of people want to trade with.

It is in that merging for posterity of country and God that no country has better searched and reached for, that this country finds its shield against the arrows of its mourners.

Could this country be demeaned and diminished all the way, having to endure in a more sophisticated manner until death happens or a sudden death is more like it for ever and ever?

The local merchants of politics do not seem to agree with the outsiders as to the sudden death of the country for they do not want to lose their country or be blamed for its loss. They are viewed more content with a long-term curtailment of the country's power and prestige as long as their special interest is served in that wheeling-dealing tabloid. The outsiders go for a touchdown of a nuclear kind on one side but do not want to offend the local merchants on the other, so they resort to a tedious hypocrisy in sniffing their way through, with their cells set in place. And who under these circumstances is more appealing than some Asians to be triggered by the merchants of people and trigger, in turn, against the United States fulfilling, thus for, the unstoppable desire of the wheeler-dealers either from the inside or the outside.?

It is specifically in this context that one should look at the various wars taking place in the Middle East after the Vietnam War and the Afghanistan War have failed to metamorphose these individual wars into a broader and wider one between Asia and the United States.

The status quo has been established with the United States as the superpower of the world on a mutual-consent basis among the two superpowers, the US and the USSR. It was a historic win over the most dangerous war, the cold war, without one drop of blood. The two superpowers have then disengaged their war option and engaged in their peace option. Such an accomplishment has astonished the world times over. This accomplishment made the merchants of people throw in their towel in recognition of an undeniable truth, the peace on Earth among people. A pragmatic president said, as a figure of speech, that "if we were told this is what was going to happen ten years ago, we would have never believed it." Another president almost lost his life in an assassination plot because he believed in peace.

Then peace started to take the back seat encouraged by enraged merchants of people who exacerbated the merits of peace in a make-believe linear politics aiming at disrupting the normal flow of peace arrangements among the great powers.

The last war in Iraq seemed to dismember most of the elements of the peace.

It remains to be seen whether the peace arrangements will hold among the big powers, but one thing had surfaced from the Iraqi war and other conflicts in the Middle East, and it is that the big powers are no more teaming together in a world policy. Since the struggle among the belligerents in the Middle East has become suicidal and sectarian, would any metamorphosis of the Middle East crises to the world be less than suicidal and sectarian?

The reminiscence of old divergences due to the lack of peace policy is sending signals of revival of the old wounds and the reshaping of history of the world wars together with a sectarianism in progress to first quell any resurgence of understanding among the major powers of the world based on the belief in one God that brought the superpowers together, with Russia opening up to its religions, and to second make the faith in God turn in a mode of extremism and extermination as if religions have become an impediment to world peace and to the stability in the world.

When the security of a country becomes a missed opportunity with sectarianism and brand politics embedded in it, who is to blame if the superpower cannot quell the sectarian fight nor can it escape the blame of the resurgence of religious civil wars?

Religious civil wars have always been detrimental to people, and it has been there as long as the differences among religions have existed, until the world came up with the separation of religion and state to alter the spread of these differences and stop this commutative problem. However, this problem is back again in a different way and form, and it is back before the world has had the chance to develop an immunization system against its new spread.

The global peacemaking policy that brought the world closer, in that it brought the superpowers in an agreement, Europe together and the Middle East in a peace outcome, and other accomplishments, was short lived, and before the ink could dry on the various treaties, preparations were under way to cut short and obliterate the peace efforts starting with the curtailment of the new superpower, whose Constitution calls for peace and transcends the differences among religions.

God's help provided for in the Constitution was also targeted and politicized.

And to accelerate the reverse process of global peace, the Pentagon and New York were hit on September 11, 2001.

The reprisal to September 11, 2001, staying in Iraq years and counting, is not helping the political vaccine and remedy against the spread of this new political germ of sectarianism of a different flux.

With the fast growing religious and political extremism, race and ethnicity, the cult of the war is not helping reduce the tensions between the parties to offset its spread locally into variances of extremism and second to correct the drive of United States versus Islam, a United States doing business as (DBA) the Christian nation.

There is no Christian nation, there is a nation with God, as well as there is no Moslem nation, there is a nation with God, and the same applies to the Jewish nation and others. And as soon as we treat religion as a nation, we cannot but enter the nationalistic sectarianism, which is another form of extremism, and the borderless nation.

In another word, there is no God with one nation or another, God is for all the people and all the nations.

God comes to the rescue when one nation that believes in him is threatened by another nation that believe in him as well, otherwise he could not be for all the people.

He wants people to connect through the process of aspiration. This process has become problematic for some because the journey to God was not construed as a live one but one after death.

In the Middle East, should the struggle becomes a three-way one with the so-called DBA Christian nation, the United States, as an intruder in the eyes of some and becoming an occupier, it should not take too much to realize who would be smacked in the middle of the battlefield, but God is there to help save those who have found themselves meddling in between in a hot pursuit.

God's help should not become politicized and construed as if it has to be channeled politically to become admissible politically, though knowledgeable by people, especially when the pretenders of canalization are the same merchants of people and by proxy want to be ones of the creator.

God has shown his help to nations and people through individuals of his choice. Moses, Jesus, Mohammad, Buddha .... These individuals were recognizable and became the witness of the people's journey to the creator. To neglect, disrespect, confuse, disturb, impoverish, hassle and harass, replace, and otherwise persecute the helpers is first to obliterate the normal process of God's help, and second to deprive the believers from undertaking their journey to him with the eye of a witness watching. Every witness watches his own flock of good believers delivering themselves to the creator.

The helper acts as an envoy from God for and by him.

The flow of believers is an uninterrupted, continuous, and contiguous one as life is, and the procreation is with the succession of people.

It takes time to develop the common obedience to God in an organized and disciplinary manner, leading to the journey to him alive from this Earth in order to transcend the differences among religions that believe in the same one God.

Any disruption of this common obedience deprives people from their salvation and induces them into a doom's status, leading to their destruction hanging on Lucifer's mercy that never comes than by means of more destruction and more doomsdays since it is Lucifer's process to get people to him.

This process would stay its course until people would have suffered enormous losses. These losses delay the healthy journey to God. People becoming doomed by destruction do not realize the realistic relief of the belief because their behavior, then flanked with pain and damages, impedes the steadiness of their basic belief, its serenity, calm, comfort, and resolute determination taking that journey to God.

Extremism is among the impediments depriving people from the common drive and the collegiality of purpose. People are torn apart, separated by the same belief in God instead of being united because of the same belief in God. And the mission entrusted into the missionaries having to deal with the dooms and destructions would lose its divine purpose since dooms and destruction are viable to Lucifer.

The persistence of people against destruction is their safe passage back again to their creator no matter what the advocates of dooms and destructions try to extract special interests from the miseries of the rest of the people. The special interest group is in no harmony with people and could not prompt itself to be more equal among the people since it has not integrated with people at the first place, and it becomes, in turn, an impediment to people.

CHAPTER 10

The Civil War

The United States has already gone through a civil war. It did cost the country a lot in terms of lives and money. It was its civil war.

Now the United States is involved in a different civil war. And it is not its war.

In its civil war, the United States was triumphant. In the Iraqi war, the United States does not seem to be triumphant.

The cost of the external Iraqi civil war is also getting bigger and depleting the Social Security funds, among others, and the borrowing is on the rise, so is the deficit. The funding for the Iraqi external war is getting difficult, the military is somehow stretched, its reputation has been targeted with some scandals and inadequate treatment of its soldiers, the presidential election is looming ahead, and it gets dirty in an election year, dirty enough to let the merchants of people vibrate their melodies of differences among the citizens, especially when a funding of its tunes is encouraged with the blame of an external civil war inflicted on the United States versed in a drift of divergences. And the whole thing is as if the United States has not fought its civil war and has not won its civil war, and in order to win, it has to win the others' civil war, or else it is defeated. You never know with the merchants of politics until you know how they change things around, inside out and upside down!

No surprise that the upside-downers, outside-inners are against any accomplishment the United States has made from winning the cold war together with then the Soviet Union, and other wars, to promoting peace and understanding, to proclaiming the civil liberties and also to winning over its civil war and other accomplishments.

The United States has been charged with a new accusation to counter its accomplishments, one of a reverse politics of achievements, and it has been brought into the trend of curtailment and the worst, but people got to be happy with what is left until it is gone, and then sorry, the United States should have known better, and this country was a dream

President Abraham Lincoln fought and won the civil war, and to pretend that the US cannot win a civil war in Iraq is to say indirectly that the US cannot win any civil war that is connected with the United State and definable as originally a civil war because if the superpower did make it in the United State, it can make it everywhere, and the reciprocal stands by a contrary judgment that if the superpower could not make it everywhere, it could not have definitely made it in the United State or it is no more the superpower of the world, and in both cases the Iraqi civil war is a prediction of what is waiting in the corridors of the merchants of people to cash in on a bestowed power to become in replacement of the existing superpower.

In other part of the Middle East, the United State is no more the major contingent of the United Nations presence, and as a matter of fact, it has no contingent at all. This situation is very indicative of what is transpiring from the Middle East that in one part of it, in Iraq, the United States has to stay there alone with one real exception, the United Kingdom, entrenched in an accrued metamorphosed civil war of the others, and in another part of the Middle East between Lebanon, Syria, and Israel, the United States is excluded from the peace forces headed by the United Nations.

The United States had not, together with the other sponsor of peace, made the peace in the Middle East a wishful thinking.

But it has been projected, carried, considered, and consumed by the extremists as if it has failed, hinted to do so by the merchants of politics in a conspiracy of a meltdown network. Those wheeler-dealers of politics that turn victory into defeat in a scheme of entrapments and triggering aided to do so by local considerations of appurtenance-based politics as if the United States had not enough from overseas impediments and misinformation to its accomplishments, its Constitution, and what it stands for, and needs to substitute the allegiance of its people to their country with a denominational appurtenance of some of them who have projected themselves above the rest of the people in a try to revamp that appurtenance decayed by partition and partisan politics on the expenses of the American people, God and Government.

The United States people's votes are not for sale, people of the superpower that trusted in God and country to make it through the perils of life successfully and thankfully so not to be subdued to a retroactive policy as if they should not have done it before they got the password to the Almighty God from the wheeler-dealers of politics connected with each other by an appurtenance they believe stronger than the allegiance, maker and breaker of presidents, and hence who needs the country since he has got the president they pretend they make and break, and who needs the allegiance since he has got the appurtenance, and who needs the president himself?

People of the United States that came from all over the world could not be against the world. If there is a country in this world whose people are from all over the world, it is the United States. Therefore, the US should not be isolated from most of the rest of the word whether in Iraq or elsewhere in the Middle East.

The United States should not become the only one country, or almost, for war, and the only one country, or almost, excluded from the peacekeepers.

This position is gaining momentum and is becoming global since the metamorphosed civil war in Iraq is described, among other descriptions, as a global war. This situation is a make-believe one and should not be interpreted as a win or loss for the United States. It is not a United States civil war to start with in order to be won or lost unless we want to make it so by the will of the entrappers mixing between sectarianism, radicalism, insurgency, terrorism, clerics, and extremism not to mention Saddamism and others to globalize it.

The merchants of politics are trying to operate a swap operation between appurtenance and allegiance, giving this country the replicas of their failure over the centuries and taking from this country its success over the years and posing as the new superpower in the horizon with the force of unhappy people.

This political traffic has become jammed and congested and all there is to it is that the United State is fighting a mixed bag of sectarianism merging from everything else because the United States had capsized Saddam Hussein's statute and he was ridden physically, but he stayed spiritually always with ammunition and money to give to the insurgents, his heirs, as well as those of his sons.

The fights between the president of US and then the president of Iraq was made personal and is still unraveling as if Saddam Hussein was still alive and his sons too and in remembrance of them and their ongoing contribution for the insurgents.

And so goes the story, when it is personal, personal money talks especially when there is a lot of it, and no place to go with it than against a personal enemy and what he personifies, and what is attached and related to or connected with, all the ideologies and projection politics, thousand stories made up out of one real story.

CHAPTER 11

Soldiers in Iraq

The mission of the United States soldiers in Iraq has to coincide with the purpose of the United States presence in Iraq, insofar as the reason for the continuous presence has yet to be defined.

It was not considered at the beginning of the war in 2003, that it would be to quell a civil war unless projections were made to fight that war as if it were a United States civil war. Such projection went from the statements thrown around of a coming conflict between the crusaders and no crusaders followed by the newspaper clips diminishing the prophet of Muslims and more than that by video clips using the United States soldiers in a scam of insulting pictures to Muslims much to the dismay and outrage of the American people and their military.

Has that projection stopped at this point?

It would not have started if it were projected to stop here. Then what is the next step?

The abuse does not stalemate and video clips have been used and could trigger a collision of a sort that could be viewed as if it were of denominational encounter whatever denominations are involved since the mood and mode of the war is a civil war.

Is the so-called civil war in Iraq contagious?

The contagion is dimensional to the number of victims it makes and could go out of proportion and control, reaching every denomination especially in an era of extremism denominational approach gaining momentum.

Soldiers are trained to fight and they do it better than anything else; they are trained to win with a permit to kill.

And short of a winnable battle on the field, would the battle move to the same barracks with video clips spreading in a spur of the moment?

This would not be a lesson of obedience on a video clip, it has not been before, neither would it be a sex scandal or a topless show, this is the use of armed forces soldiers and means for a purpose contrary to the teaching of allegiance for country and God.

The purpose for which the Iraqi war is going on is on the loose. And since no real purpose has limited the Iraqi war, the war expands. The projections were for an expansion beyond the limits of Iraq and the Middle East, including the conflict between the Palestinians and the Israelis, to one between the US and Asia. However, this escalation is not easily attainable due to the reserve of alert politics carried over from the peace era and the peacekeeping politics. People of goodwill have not given up on their accomplishments and believe in the betterment of the humans under God.

And until these projections of a regional and continental conflicts become attainable, the wars in Iraq and elsewhere in the Middle East are sought by the merchants of politics and intended to stay for whatever give-and-take reasons unless it could trigger an interior and local issue inside each continent to induce more in a conflict between the continents.

The weakening of each continent is also sought by the merchants of politics to become a factor inciting the other continent to seize an opportunity to prevail, and until the weakening process has not yielded yet to a confrontation, the Iraqi war keeps developing and its description keeps getting broader as well as its costs.

The question that imposes itself is how the Iraqi war keeps going; should it not have become a civil war?

It looks as if the Iraqi war has exhausted every other reason for its being, or almost has, except for the reason of sectarianism, so sectarianism is not projected to end soon. Casualties are mounting, the tools of war are also increasing, and the costs of war are on the rise, and so on.

The United States seems to be waiting on a crossroad for the green light to exit Iraq. Its people want that exit, while some of its politicians do not seem in a hurry. They are taking their time caught in a crossfire, and the unease of its people is growing.

These politicians are wondering why their plight for democracy is not taken at its face value.

There is no plight for democracy in the war in Iraq but one against democracy. Sectarianism and democracy do not go hand in hand. The separation of church and state has been at the flash of democracy.

Also, the touch of personal and local politics does give ways to a surge of new attitudes incompatible with the normal run of democracy and public matters.

Democracy is opposed to personal, what public interest is to sectarianism.

The personal considerations lie in the analysis of personality and the repercussion the personal could have on the public. In the Vietnam War, for example, President Nixon's personal preference in foreign policy laid the ground for an end to the Vietnam War that was felt more and more in the country with a growing belly for religious differences. It is a question of personal conviction and tactics. Also, Vietnam War could not stand against the surge of international understanding. Not even the cold war could stand against such understanding. It was the foreign policy of President Nixon that saved him from impeachment and indictment.

It was the wisdom of the peacemaking politicians, believers in Constitution, country, and God, that carried over the making of the United States as the superpower of the world. It was in that political enclave that the peaceful repression of local politics of denominational ingredients because of the Vietnam War, was successful and the apprehensions were gone because the Vietnam War was gone.

Is President Bush's foreign policy in the line of conduct of his predecessors that have backed the peacemaking policy leading to the superpower ship of the United State in the world with the world accepting?

The answer does not seem encouraging for President Bush, according to the polls and the votes, nationally and internationally. So if President Nixon ended the war in Vietnam, would President Bush do it in Iraq to offset an ongoing resentment among the citizens and in particular the victims of the Iraqi war and what would transpire out of it or triggered by it, God forbid.

CHAPTER 12

The War's Outcome

It is imperative that first, we define the belligerent parties in the war, in other words, who is who.

To set the superpower on an equal foot with terrorists and/or insurgents is quite frankly diminishing the superpower militarily, having to fight a loose network of insurgents on the run revolting against the superpower in a contagious approach of defiance, inviting contenders and competitors to cash in on the debacle.

It is equally curtailing the superpower by dragging its feet in a civil religious war while its Constitution is basically against such an enticement since it reflects God's love for all the people who believe in him regardless of their worship denomination. The United States has successfully avoided and aborted a religious civil war because it is against the Constitution and its reach for perfection of a nation of the brave in the land of the free too close to their creator the closeness of God's mission on Earth.

Therefore, to be indulged and pushed into a religious civil war is to dismember the teamwork with and under God that the Constitution has evolved around, and any inducement of the United States into a religious civil war becomes unconstitutional according to the spirit and letter of the Constitution.

It is that closeness of God, country, and people that had worried the extremists in a network of bidders for God's preferred treatment alarmed and pushed away by the prime time of the Constitution.

It is in the compound of worship of one God for all away from the turbulences of the religious civil war that the country keeps securing its prime stand with God and hence in the world.

The world looks up at the superpower as second to God, and this superpower does not and should not fight among believers to prove who is who, but bring believers together, since the almighty had already bonded its Constitution and its people with his help, and also, the superpower status in a time record of divine purposes as everything in this world has a divine purpose.

The war in Iraq has become a religious civil war, no matter what the warriors of negations want to call it. Therefore, to fight a denomination's followers of a religion (Sunnis), and another denomination's followers of the same religion (Shiites), is to fight the religion itself since this religion is mainly and overwhelmingly made out of these two denominations' followers.

Religious wars are sentimentally intense especially when the right to die for a religion seems to supersede a prohibition to fight a brother in faith let alone of the same religion.

And the question becomes what could it supersede next?

It is hardly doubtful that it does not supersede everything else since for many followers of Islam, death in the Iraqi war supersedes life on this Earth for the reward of heaven.

It is in this context of death reward leading all the way to death by all kinds of weapons with no consideration for a stoppage that religious wars should be avoided.

The Iraqi war could not be taken away from the Middle East conflict and context, a Middle East engulfed in religious discordances, taboos, fights, wars after wars, and thereafter until death takes the parties apart. The Iraqi religious war is igniting the wick of the Middle East time bomb while the superpower that has helped to diffuse that time bombshell is becoming itself more and more of an isolated party at war after having been a successful sponsor of peace with another superpower and the breaker of peace driven by its Constitution and what it stands for under God.

peace with another superpower and the breaker of peace driven by its Constitution and what it stands for under God.

CHAPTER 13

The Nuclear

With the superpowers getting together in the 1980s and the voluntary dissolution of the Soviet Union leaving the United States the only superpower in the world, everything was set for the control of the nuclear. There was no more a race for the supremacy of one power over the other one, the reduction of the nuclear arsenal was elaborated with first reductions of weapons of mass destruction, the nonproliferation of the nuclear weapons was an established policy, the world was moving softly but swiftly towards the regulations and processes of understandings among the nations talking to each other not at each other, the templates of peace were set to last in the new establishment proven to win the wars, even the cold war, through the force of the word.

The world was getting closer by the day with the progress of communication taking the lead in the computer world.

In other words, the world had everything it takes to move forward, making it a better place to live and its people a happier people to be.

It was proper for the world's new establishment to embrace more the belief in God as the source of comfort and happiness, and it did with the old Soviet Bloc embracing again its prior religions leading to God, and China engaging in democratization with a sympathy for the worship of God.

It was the end of an old era and the beginning of a new one characterized with an everlasting splash of hope to live in peace away from war. And although some incidents and limited confrontations have indented the peace process, the peacemaking policy was the rule among nations.

The build-up of peace took a negative turn with the resurgence of a network of profiteers unhappy with the peace process. And in order to implement the expansion of war, the superpowers became targeted until September 11, 2001, put a cap on the peace process. A secretive network that was dormant during the peace years became more active, imploring the necessity of war, encouraged by a network made of all kind of pieces gathering the unhappy complainers, the too close to call, the avengers of their destiny, the prospectors in replacement of the superpowers status-quo, and the terrorists who were put in the front row.

It goes to say that in that network, every element is seeking his own hegemony in his own environment to start with, but all the network is seeking damage to the superpower, and this is what is keeping the pieces of the network together around a common cause.

This situation has been shown in particular with the nuclear proliferation issue, as if the issue of acquiring nuclear power is for the purpose of defending oneself against the superpower.

The common ground and cause is formed, and that is to be against the superpower, remains what the wheeling-dealing among the elements of the network, gathered against the superpower, could produce, especially when some in that network do possess the nuclear and are tempted with the price offered by those who have it not to acquire it.

The mistake to stay in Iraq is one that had generated into almost a full isolation of the superpower, helped with a policy of alienation resulting from a special interest group-based politics incoherent with an allegiance, and the whole thing bracketed into a lunatic and stubborn overview, giving more reason for the network to sustain its course.

The nonproliferation of the nuclear weapon has cherished so many people of goodwill, but has become subdued and almost substituted with the no deployment of weapons of mass destruction as if the proliferation is a done deal phase of the nuclear and now we have entered the phase of its deployment control.

The spirit of the Constitution centered around the more perfect union under God forbids either the race or the proliferation of nuclear weapons let alone their deployment.

The trust in God is the salvation of all humans and not the mistrust in humans in their race for nuclear deployment that could lead to the salvation of some humans and makes a breed survive, if any, on the expenses of the other.

There is God not without humans and they have to reach for him. And there are humans not without God should they become more perfect. And there is God's help to witness the journey of humans alive to the creator and the salvation of humans pertaining from their trust in God, the creator, the giver, the savior, the life itself that nuclear could not and should not take away now that almost the whole world has become believers and there is no segregation among believers and no more equals than others since we are talking about the life of people and people are created equal, and God is for all.

CHAPTER 14

The Human Nature

The Constitution has embraced, among other philosophies, the notion that a human being is born innocently good but society depraves him.

The question becomes how could society deprave him or her had he or she not been predisposed to divert from goodness?

Those who have ended with the conclusion that the human being is born without necessarily a good nature in him, have, in order to correct the human nature, addressed the subject from the standpoint of the remedy conducive to punishment and damage to bear both physically and monetarily. And since the damages of retribution seemed lucrative to those who have applied them to others, they became addicted to them and more so to the extent that the more damage, the more is the retribution, and the more is the retribution, the more doomed are the people that have to endure.

This punishment recipe stems from the fact that those who inflict punitive damages should be worst than the born-bad people if any, and they could not be but worst since they are seekers of the more equal among people deciding about the human nature , with the right to lucrative punishment of the common people.

In this order of quality from bad to worst, it has become obvious that those who have embraced the worst order believe they have got it made since it is the worst that wins in a negative order of quality. And it remains how many folds of the worst could the humans embrace all the way to nuclear deployment?

To this, the impulse of an answer for the adherents to the philosophy of badness trend, up till now, is that they will cross the bridge when they come to it. In the meantime, their policy of punitive damages is still lucrative enough or, so to speak, and that is what matters to them, until the time wherein they will blow the whistle or ring the bell as to blowing the horn in time of war, only it is a war not like the others and the punitive damages might be much greater all the way to a change of the world status quo. And so the status quo has got to be changed once and for all. It is as if they were asking to be a onetime winner in order to become an all-time winner, all in one!

A human is born with goodness and in his creator's image. Infants are the image of innocence and love. And as life goes on, a human reaches a stage of puberty and adolescence desirable enough to tempt him or her away from and against adults of prior generations.

It is in that temptation that the confusion among remedies has exacerbated the minds of philosophers. And instead of saying now it is for God to take over in order to win over the temptation in that direct relation between each individual and God, the interceptors stepped in and assumed the role of God in the form of punitive damages..

Adam and Eve were tempted and they had to answer to God. Never even evil did take on himself the task of punishing them on the assumption that they were bad by birth.

The salvation of human beings is through the belief in one God and not through the processes of punishments, for the pardon is divine and the win over evil is with God's help, and the temptation is originally excluded from trying the divine power.

Peace has always been the answer for good people to live together. If there were not good people, there would not have been peace among nations and people. And since there has been peace in the world, there have been good people.

The peacemaking policy has proven that the world could live in peace, and it has won over the cold war without one drop of blood. A big sigh of relief has overcome every fear of doubt and uncertainty.

The pursuit of peace is a conditional requirement for a good policy, and there is a good policy compared to a bad policy, as there is public interest compared to personal interest. A personal interest-directed policy leads ineluctably to bad policy, which in turn leads to war.

Peace is and always has been and always will be the good answer to wars no matter whether the predicaments, means, and ways of war are: nuclear, chemical, biological, and conventional. Peace at a time of nuclear age is more needed than at any time before. And it is more so when a war is one of concepts and abstracts, misinformation and disinformation, ideologies and projections.

Those who will try to find any answer to change a war line policy than with a peace line policy are wasting the taxpayers' life and money and taking people's happiness away, engaging people in a doom-and-destruction policy to bear and endure.

Simply stated, there is no substitute for peace than peace. Neither is peace the reason for war, nor war the reason for peace per say. Peace stands for and by itself; it is a trend and a way of life, a pursuance to reach a divine purpose. All religions turn around the peace for an answer to their well-being, and among all the acclamation words for the lord Jesus, one has always emerged flamboyant: "king of peace."

CHAPTER 15

The UFO

Odorless,
Soundless,
Bright light moving across the sky
High as much as the eye can see
And low as to hide behind the tree,
Harmless,
Visitor of kindness, hope and peace,
From the other world to this world.

Has history given enough merits to Jesus, who physically descended from the sky and appeared unto others?

Jesus has been loved because of his unique and immense goodness and also because he was the "in between" at almost equal distance between the creator and people, divine and human.

Jesus made his presence known to the humans. He is the light, the guiding light for those who want to take the path of light, and he is the shining light that could move mountains and seas from one to another one by the force of believe in God. Although he is a human, his life on Earth has not always been as a human, and although he is divine, his life has not always been as the divine Father.

And even though he is a spirit, his presence on Earth was not only spiritual. He was on Earth to provide a living physical proof of what the divine can do and what the humans are in constant need to be done through divinity.

Jesus has not, with his resurrection, detached himself definitely physically from the humans' Earth. He wanted to keep his divine communication with the Father enforced, loud and clear, resonating through the universe, from Earth to the infinite, a universe that the humans are trying to explore, and the communication is going on encouraged and maintained by Jesus.

The UFO appearances are a show of a divine, supernatural power. And with these proofs of the supernatural, humans need indoctrination, some time a one-on-one dialogue, and hence the many other forms of God's help through his picked beloved ones who he gives a kind of delegation of power.

Jesus has been dotted with both powers, supernatural and word, and it was too much for some humans, then, to digest the mix; therefore, there is through divinity the supernatural and through humanity the force of the word that God Almighty gives so gracefully to those he picks with his unparalleled humbleness in a temporary delegation of power of the word. I have witnessed that grace and humbleness. Thanks to gracious God, I am a believer.

I was born in 1940 in the Ivory Coast during the Second World War. I grew up to become an attorney. Prayers were an essential part of my life. I would not have made it then or now without my constant salute to the creator. I started with long hours of prayers every day, especially before important days in my life, and I knew that one day God Almighty would answer me. As a matter of fact, I was so sure that God would answer my prayers that I never doubted it. And one day, he did. And ever since that day, his help became more known to me on a constant basis.

My experience has proven to me that once connected with God, you tangibly know it and you are in there for an indefinite time, always connected, and you are there for the long run, the sky's the limit.

The house where I was raised has a long deck. I used to take a walk on that deck forward and backward hundreds of time, inventing prayers to God, adding to the existing prayers adjectives of praise, love, and respect to the Almighty, always determined to keep on like never before. His presence was felt not as if it were an online chat but it directs me to win real challenges, and I felt the invincibility in him. Never have I wanted to relinquish the grasp of a winner believer and the joy to hold to it was always compensated with more tangible enjoyment challenges' rewards given to me by the creator. I felt that Eucharistic celebration from a giving God to a human taker, as to say: "Take, be happy, do it, I can make you so."

To me, God is a giver to those who ask him with determination. As to those who do not want to see or hear the truth, I feel sorry for them, for they do not know what they are missing: the truth.

CHAPTER 16

The Coming

Among religions, there are those who believe that the messiah is not the Jesus that they knew. There are those who believe that the same Jesus is coming back, and there are those who believe that God has turned the page on a new corner stone of belief. These divergences have wasted too much time and energy, let alone blood of the people that believe in the same God.

Who among the believers in the same God would want more waste?

No one in his sane mind would want that, certainly not in these dying ages with the uncertainty of the no deployment of the weapons of mass destruction.

Then, there should be definitely a common ground where the believers could and should stand on. Creation is not a waste after millenniums of constant drive to gather around the belief in God.

Indeed, there is a common ground to stand on should we read the teachings of God and his picked beloved ones carefully with the eyes of real believers.

Let's take the example of Jesus:

First of all, it would be too much to believe that the Virgin Mary went through a normal conception, as is the case among humans. God created the human without the conception of the human. He does not need that for a divine enlightening witness

Second, it would be troublesome to believe that Jesus has never existed before 2,000 years ago, for he is in the minds of many believers, divine and hence, eternal, and eternal means he has always existed.

Then, how could the divine operate to bring to the humans somebody like them, born and raised all the way to death, wherein the divine clearly picks up and takes over again in a definite mutation, certainly not difficult for God to do.

As it is true that God could raise a human from death, it is equally true that God could bring death and the dead human body be carried until he meets the mother that is already ready to accept him in the form of a baby consecrating the birth to life.

Who would do the carrying?

God's help would do the carrying message for he is trusted with the mother who is told to trust in him.

Would a human, God's help carrier, picked by God be involved after the birth to human life of the divine?

Nobody will ever know as much as everybody knows the birth to human life of the divine is not through regular human means.

There are things that a human has not, could not, and will not understand about God's divinity. The original bounties from God to Adam and Eve have been revoked because of the temptations to equal divinity, and the humans had to sweat for their daily bread.

Those who are making the human sweat more, elevating themselves to a more equal status by imposing punitive damages onto the others, are not making it easier on the humans; on the contrary, they are prophesizing the doom people for a destructive policy.

The fact remains that if God Almighty has decided that humans should sweat forever and this is to be the destiny of the humans pursued by punitive damages from humans to humans, it would have been self-defeating with the heavenly father paradise set to accept humans, and with the spread of the belief and its corner stones and pardon remedies to gather the people of the world in their journey to the creator alive from this earth. In other words, death will not be needed to meet the creator, and the humans are redeemed in paradise.

Therefore, humans had to go through a labor period acquiring the notion of obedience and respect to God, accepting him as the one and only, the Almighty to the extent that no one could be tempted to aspire to his unique status before and after his grace is rekindled again to the humans.

No one, indeed, not even Jesus that had to reaffirm the unique power and universal infinite status of the creator by leaving the human doubtful condition with the request not to forsake him being deprived from the water of life and given the vinegar of death.

The expectation of the new comer is tied up with the conditions of people relevant to accept the creator as the one and unique God no matter who is the new corner stone, no matter the form since the substance is the same in meeting the creator alive, no need for intermediaries any more, they are only witnesses.

The United States Constitution has touched base with the people's inner right to take the journey to their creator, as people, regardless of their religions and other differences. People are endowed with certain inalienable rights and the launch pad for the journey to the creator was set and God's help was invoked not as an offense to the decision-makers of the country but as a defense of people against the endurances of bad decisions of some politicians..

It is *the People; We the People.*

Should the new world, the new spirit, the new deal, the new establishment fail in fulfilling the expectations of people's drive to meet their creator, then we can wait for a repeat performance of Jesus, at the place of Jesus, a rebirth of the mechanism of performances and miracles until people are ready to proclaim more and more the unchallenged one God in a revamp, unwavering belief in him, to take the journey, the final crossing to him, direct as they may and should by then, at the example and teaching of enlightening born/ born again, old/new Jesus.